Riding
the
School Bus
with
Mrs.
Kramer

written by
ALICE K. FLANAGAN

photographs by
CHRISTINE OSINSKI

Reading Consultant
LINDA CORNWELL
Learning Resource Consultant
Indiana Department of Education

CHILDREN'S PRESS®   *A Division of Grolier Publishing*
New York • London • Hong Kong • Sydney • Danbury, Connecticut

Special thanks to Debra Kramer
for allowing us to tell her story.

Author's Note:
Mrs. Kramer's last name is pronounced KRAY-mer.

Library of Congress Cataloging-in-Publication Data
Flanagan, Alice.
  Riding the school bus with Mrs. Kramer / written by Alice K.
Flanagan ; photographs by Christine Osinski ; reading consultant, Linda
Cornwell.
       p. cm. — (Our neighborhood series)
  Summary: Text and photographs follow Mrs. Kramer, a safe and
careful bus driver, as she gets the children to school on time and brings
them home again at the end of the day.
  ISBN 0-516-20779-2 (lib. bdg.)   0-516-26406-0 (pbk.)
  1. Bus drivers—Juvenile literature. [1. Bus drivers. 2. Occupations.]
I. Osinski, Christine, ill. II. Title. III. Series: Our neighborhood (New
York, N.Y.)
HD8039.M8F58 1998
388.3'22—dc21   97-32645
                                                       CIP
                                                       AC

Photographs ©: Christine Osinski

Hurry up! Don't be late.
The school bus is here.

Say hello
to Mrs. Kramer.

Every morning, she drives children to school. In the afternoon, she brings them home again.

Everyone knows Mrs. Kramer. She has been driving a school bus for eighteen years.

Mrs. Kramer likes to be around children. On her bus, she knows each child by name.

She listens to them talk about their problems. She hears all about the funny things that happen to them.

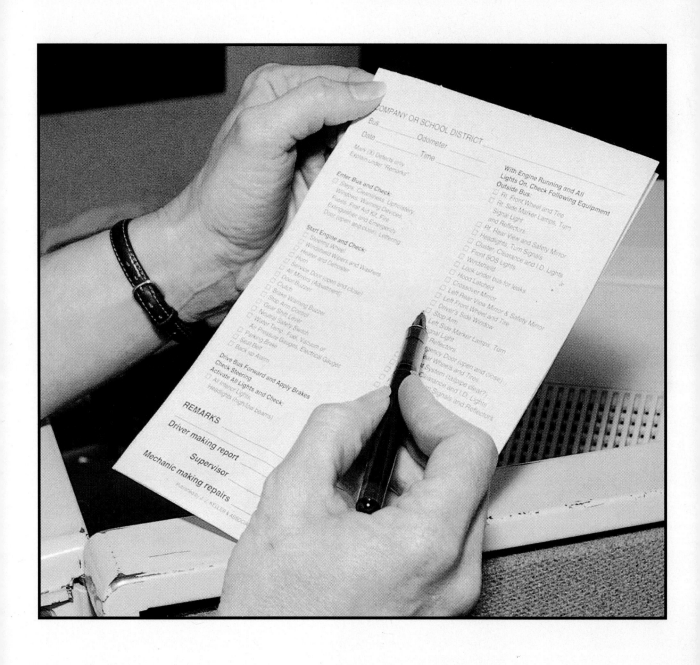

Mrs. Kramer is a safe driver.

Before taking out the bus each day, she does a safety check.

Is the first-aid kit in place?
Will the fire extinguisher work?

Does the emergency door open and close?

Mrs. Kramer listens to the engine.
She works the wipers, the horn,
the lights, and the brakes.

Then she checks the tires and the mirrors. The bus is ready to go.

Safety is always important.
Before Mrs. Kramer stops
to pick up children or let
them off, she turns on the
bus's yellow warning lights.

After the bus comes to a complete
stop, she turns on the red flashing
lights.

She opens the bus door. She looks out her left window to be sure her stop sign goes out.

Other drivers see it and stop. Then
the children can cross the street safely.

Sometimes, Mrs. Kramer must drive in bad weather, such as fog, snow, rain, and sleet. And sometimes the roads are winding.

On the trip to and from school, Mrs. Kramer makes sure the children behave and stay in their seats.

At a railroad crossing, Mrs. Kramer stops the bus fifteen feet from the tracks.

She listens for a whistle and looks for a train. Everything must be clear before she can cross!

Several times a day, Mrs. Kramer calls the office on her CB radio. She tells her boss, Mr. Ferrar, just where she is.

Every year, Mrs. Kramer and
Mr. Ferrar teach safety rules to
the children.

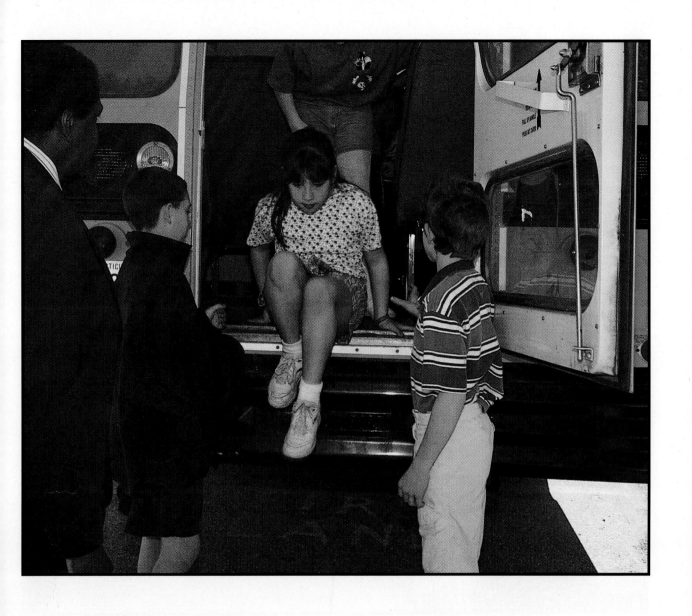

The children practice using the emergency exits. In case the bus is in an accident, they need to know how to get off the bus.

Driving a school bus is a very important job. Twice a day, children's lives are in Mrs. Kramer's care.

Teachers count on Mrs. Kramer to get the children to school on time.

29

Parents depend on Mrs. Kramer to get their children to school safely and bring them home again.

Meet the Author
and the Photographer

Alice Flanagan and Christine Osinski are sisters. They grew up together telling stories and drawing pictures in a brown brick bungalow in a southwest-side neighborhood of Chicago, Illinois. Today they write stories and take photographs professionally.

Ms. Flanagan resides in Chicago with her husband and works as a freelance writer. Ms. Osinski is a photographer and teaches at The Cooper Union for the Advancement of Science and Art in New York City. She lives with her husband and two sons in Ridgefield, Connecticut.